The
Christian

T5-CCJ-591

DESCRIBED

The Key Truth *A Christian is a person who has received Jesus Christ as Savior and Lord and has submitted to the rule of God's kingdom.*

A sinner saved by grace

It was at Antioch that believers in Christ were first called *Christians*— probably as a term of abuse. However, Christians have always valued this identification, because of the immensity of the debt they owe to Christ, after whom they are called.

It is God's grace that has brought the sinner into union with Christ. Grace is the free, unearned favor of God toward the sinner. This grace is only possible because of the Cross, and it is made real to us by the Holy Spirit. Salvation cannot be earned: it is a free gift to be received by faith.

SINNER (Acts 11:26; Ephesians 2:8, 9; 1 Timothy 1:15) As a Christian, you are a sinner saved by grace. Using these verses, how would you restate this truth?

A member of God's family

In his letter to the Roman Christians, the apostle Paul teaches that the people who did not belong to God at all are now, by His grace, called sons of the living God.

Such a title is not naturally ours. It is only given to those who receive Jesus Christ. It is by the power of God's love that this "adoption" into His family takes place. Being part of the church means to learn the discipline and joy of being in the family.

MEMBER (Romans 9:25, 26; John 1:12, 13; Ephesians 3:14, 15) As a Christian, you are a member of God's family. Using these verses, how would you restate this truth?

A disciple of Jesus Christ

A "disciple" in Jesus' day was a person who followed both his master's teaching and his way of life. Christ said that those who were willing to love *Him* and obey Him first above all else were His disciples. A Christian is a person who has responded to His call, "Follow Me".

DISCIPLE (Luke 14:26, 27; Matthew 9:9) As a Christian, you are a disciple of Jesus Christ. Using these verses, what should a true disciple's attitude be?

A temple of the Holy Spirit

In the Old Testament, the Jews were given special instructions on how to build the temple—and on it they lavished all their riches, craftsmanship and care, so that God should be glorified in every possible way. In his letter to the Corinthians, Paul tells us that our bodies are the temple of the Holy Spirit. This means that all our abilities and powers should be devoted towards glorifying God.

> *TEMPLE (1 Kings 6; Acts 7:48, 49; 1 Corinthians 6:19, 20) As a Christian, you are the temple of the Holy Spirit. Using these verses, what should your attitude be and what is your responsibility?*

A pilgrim in an alien environment

Many of the Old Testament's great figures are described as people who had no permanent home of their own. Abraham, for example, left the security of his family home to live in tents in a foreign land. The writer to the Hebrews describes such people as those who saw that the earth was not their home. Similarly, the New Testament urges us not to put our trust in material possessions, and to guard against a lack of discipline. For we too must realize that this earth is not our true home. Christians are like foreigners and strangers, with their permanent home elsewhere.

> *PILGRIM (Exodus 22:21; Hebrews 11:8-16; 1 Peter 2:11, 12) As a Christian you are a pilgrim in an alien environment. Using these verses, how would you restate this truth?*

A citizen of heaven

The Christian will not find permanence in this earthly existence; the permanent city still lies in the future. But the full membership and many of the privileges of that better city are with every Christian now.

As a result, the Christian is described as a citizen of heaven. We see ourselves as people who belong to another country—and we are ambassadors of that country while we live on earth.

> *CITIZEN (Ephesians 2:19; Hebrews 13:14; Revelation 22:14) As a Christian you are a citizen of heaven. What does that mean to you now? What will it mean in the future?*

Reflection Point: *This lesson "describes" you as a Christian. In which areas do you need great amounts of growth? How will you achieve that growth?*

Thought Starters

1. Study Ephesians 2:1-10, 19. Reflect on the "but" of verse 4. In what way is it the shaft of light that illuminates the passage? If you were going to speak on verses 8 and 9, what major points would you make?

2. Two descriptions of the Christian are given in Ephesians 2:19. To what extent have you experienced the privileges implied by these terms?

3. What are the insecure aspects of being a Christian? What are the secure aspects?

4. Try to think of some less prominent biblical illustrations of the Christian, and what they imply. (Clue: use 2 Timothy 2.)

FURTHER STUDY

From your study of this lesson, list two descriptions of a Christian that you would like to study further. Beside each description, give at least one scripture verse from this or another study that you will use to begin your study.

"...doing the will of God from your heart" (Ephesians 6:6). Jungfraujoch, Switzerland

THE CHRISTIAN AND THE BIBLE

The Key Truth *Through the Bible, the Christian comes to an understanding of God's plan and receives nourishment for Christian living.*

THE BIBLE

Directs the Christian for life

Biblically, a disciple of Jesus is recognized by unashamed loyalty to Christ's person and unquestioning obedience to His commands. The Master cannot accept disciples who want to establish their own method of instruction or set their own course.

Jesus taught that those obedient to His words would be characterized by stability; the disobedient would be overthrown. This is a principle throughout Scripture. *The Bible is like a lamp, guiding the Christian.*

DIRECTS (John 8:31, 32; Matthew 7:24-27; Psalm 119:105) What would Christianity be like if Christians saw the Bible as a book of "suggestions"?

Equips the Christian for battle

The believer must learn from Christ, who resisted the Devil's temptations in the wilderness with His knowledge of the Old Testament. A working knowledge of the Bible is a weapon of spiritual power.

Equally, in defending the Christian faith, the Christian who enters the arena having thought through the issues beforehand is at an immense advantage. A biblically-trained mind is a weapon of priceless value. *The Bible is like a sword, protecting the Christian.*

EQUIPS (Matthew 4:1-11; Ephesians 6:17) What happens to us in the midst of Satan's attacks when we have not been faithful in spending time studying God's Word?

Energizes the Christian for service

The disciple is called to be fruitful in service, bringing both the compassion and challenge of Christ's message to bear upon a needy world.

It is the inexhaustible supply found in God's living Word that gives Christian service its vitality and freshness. The Bible's depths can never be plumbed. *The Bible is like water, renewing the Christian.*

ENERGIZES (John 15:16; Isaiah 55:10, 11; Psalm 1) What happens if a Christian attempts to serve God without renewing himself through God's Word?

Corrects the Christian in error

The Bible exposes and corrects many errors and distortions of true belief. There is the *legalist*—the victim of convention; the empty *ritualist*—the victim of superstition; the *traditionalist*—the victim of pride; the *rationalist*—the victim of unbelief; and the mere *theorist*—the victim of laziness.

The Bible is God's message to us. Because of this, we should always be open to it to correct our own wrong ideas, and to replace them with God's truth. *The Bible is like a mirror, reforming the Christian.*

CORRECTS (Isaiah 29:13; Mark 7:9-13; James 1:23-25) Do you see yourself in any of the above descriptions? If not, can you name one area in which the Bible has corrected an error on your part?

Develops the Christian in the faith

The Bible is food for every Christian. We are called upon to grow up from spiritual childhood, strengthened by God's Word.

As we advance toward maturity, we should be able to see the great themes of Scripture as a connected whole, rather than as a collection of scattered thoughts. *The Bible is like milk, nourishing the Christian.*

DEVELOPS (2 Timothy 2:15; 1 Corinthians 14:20; 1 Peter 2:2, 3) What is the most recent way in which the Bible is developing you to maturity in Christ?

Informs the Christian of God's mind

The Bible is God's written revelation. It is impossible to arrive at a knowledge of His plan and will on the strength of our own guesswork. God has given us the Bible so that we should not be in the dark about who He is, and what He is doing.

The true wisdom that leads to salvation is arrived at by a humble and careful study of God's Word. *The Bible is like treasure, enriching the believer.*

INFORMS (Romans 11:33-36; 2 Timothy 3:14, 15; Psalm 119:162) Why did God make it impossible for man to know His will apart from His written revelation?

Reflection Point: *To develop a balanced faith, the Christian should read the Bible regularly and thoroughly. Unless we read all of the Bible, we may distort or overemphasize some aspect of its message. Is your current study of the Bible balanced? What is your remedy?*

Thought Starters

1. Read 2 Timothy 3:14-4:5. What is the nature of the Bible's power, and what does it achieve? What can regular readers expect it to do in their lives? What are the dangers which may be avoided through the Bible's message?

2. What would be a good plan and schedule for the reading of the Bible? What plans have your friends found helpful?

3. Why is it vital to become mature in the truth of the Bible? Compare your findings with Acts 20:29-32.

4. Read Psalm 19:7-11. Try to list the ways in which the writer of this Psalm delights in God's Word, and make the passage a subject for praising God.

FURTHER STUDY

From your study of this lesson, determine your personal plan and schedule for reading the Bible. Write it below and make your starting date a covenant with God.

"You are my refuge and my shield; I have put my hope in Your Word" (Psalm 119:114). Caernarvon Castle, North Wales

THE CHRISTIAN AND PRAYER

The Key Truth *Prayer is God's chosen way of communication and fellowship between the Christian and Himself. It is the secret of spiritual growth and effective service.*

PRAYER IS ESSENTIAL

For communion with God

Christian prayer is not a technique. To try to manipulate God for our own purposes is the way of magic and of the old cultic religions—when man is at the center. With Christian prayer God is at the center.

On the human level, we do not like to use those whom we love—and the same is true of those who have entered into a relationship with God of trust and acceptance. Jesus taught His friends to talk to God as to their heavenly Father and not to use meaningless incantations characteristic of heathen worship, for prayer involves a relationship. We should learn from the example of Jesus, who would regularly go away and spend time alone with His Father.

> *COMMUNION (Matthew 6:5-8; Mark 1:35; Luke 5:15, 16) Is your prayer life real communion with God? How can you help it to be more of a real communion with Him?*

For growth in God

Prayer is like breathing in the life of a Christian. When we pray regularly, what takes place in our lives is a steady growth in character and inner resources. Contrary to popular opinion, prayer is not a sign of weakness, but of strength and progress.

Prayer is an education. The disciples needed to be taught by Jesus, and He gave them a pattern of prayer that the Church has never forgotten. The Christian of every age faces the same lessons, disciplines and privileges of growing in God.

> *GROWTH (Ephesians 3:14-19; Matthew 6:9-13) Is your prayer life aiding your spiritual growth? Your growth of character and inner resources? How can you help it to be more effective in this area?*

For the service of God

God does not need our prayers. Prayer does not affect His will and overall purpose for us. But the Bible teaches, and our Christian experience confirms, that prayer does affect His specific actions in fulfilling His will.

The reason is that God has appointed prayer as a key way of *involving* His people in the carrying out of His will and service in this world. The Christian learns to pray in the name of Jesus—that is, with His interests at heart. He also learns to pray with the help of the Holy Spirit. Prayer is the most important form of service we can ever employ.

SERVICE (James 5:16-18; Ephesians 6:18) Is your prayer life effective in His service? What would help it to be more effective?

For the praise of God

The Christian is a temple of the Holy Spirit, and is therefore to glorify God in everything. Thanksgiving, joy and praise are key aspects in a Christian's attitude, according to the New Testament.

To praise God is to make great affirmations about Him. This is evident in the book of Psalms, in which we repeatedly read of God's greatness and of what He has done for His people. As we meditate on the great themes of the Bible, so our praise of God becomes a vital part of prayer.

PRAISE (1 Thessalonians 5:16-18; Psalm 34:1-3) Is your prayer life characterized by joy and praise of God? What would encourage true joy and praise in your prayers?

For the experience of God

Prayer can bring God into the heart of every human emotion and experience. The writers of the Psalms were able to look to God for guidance in times of uncertainty. The apostles were able to turn to Him in praise and prayer when in prison. Paul was strengthened by God, even though His prayer for relief from affliction was not granted. Prayer allows God to mold and develop the new man in Jesus Christ.

EXPERIENCE (Psalm 57:1-3; Acts 16:22-25; 2 Corinthians 12:7-10) Do your prayers make God real to you in every situation? In which situations is it more difficult to sense His presence? What can you do to encourage the reality of His presence through your prayers?

Reflection Point: *There is a particular power and the promised presence of Christ when believers meet together to pray in His name—according to the promise of Matthew 18:19, 20. Do you believe that promise? Do you always act as though you do? Why or why not?*

Thought Starters

1. Think about the Lord's prayer as recorded in Matthew 6:9-13. What pattern does it set for us in our prayer life? What similar patterns have you established in your own praying?

2. Why bother to pray? List some convincing reasons.

3. Why do most people find prayer not the easiest of activities? How can we help one another in this?

4. A Scottish preacher has said, "We have actually got it all wrong when we speak as we do about praying for the work, because prayer *is* the work." How do you react to this statement?

FURTHER STUDY

From your study of this lesson, list two aspects of prayer you would like to study further. Beside each listing, give at least one Scripture verse you will use to begin your study.

"And the peace of God... will guard your hearts and minds in Christ Jesus" (Philippians 4:7). Oahu, Hawaii

THE CHRISTIAN AND WITNESS

The Key Truth *Christian witness is the means by which God, through His servants, continues the work of His Son in bringing the message of salvation to the world.*

Proclaiming a person

Because Christianity is concerned with a Person rather than with a philosophy or religious system, the early disciples of Christ found little difficulty in witnessing. Whatever their education or background, they had all experienced the transforming power of the risen Christ.

Their witness was about Him—and so Philip on the desert road spoke of Jesus to the Ethiopian official. This means that all who obey Jesus as Lord have something to share. Every Christian is a witness.

PERSON (Acts 1:8; 8:35; Luke 24:46-48) As twentieth century Christians, we did not live and walk with Jesus while He was on earth. Can you explain why we are to be bold and enthusiastic witnesses as the early disciples were?

Explaining the truth

While it is Christ we proclaim, there are, however, important facts in the Christian message which must be explained and understood if individuals are to become more than mere converts. The apostle Paul's aim was that men and women should grow to become spiritually mature in Christ.

In societies where there is little awareness of God or the Bible, it is vital that the truth be taught, defended and explained.

TRUTH (Colossians 1:28, 29; Acts 18:4; 2 Timothy 2:2) Why are some Christians afraid to share reasons for their faith with skeptics?

Sharing a love

Behind the message of reconciliation is the motivating power of Christ's love. Christ sends us out into the world not merely to talk about Him, but to share His love and our love with others. Paul said that he preached because he was compelled by the love of Christ.

LOVE (2 Corinthians 5:14; 1 Thessalonians 2:7-13) Are you compelled by the love of Christ to make Him known to others? How do you respond to the love of Christ?

Witnessing consistently

Jesus said that the mark of His disciples was to be the presence of love in their fellowship. Their lives were to shine as lights in the world, through their words, their deeds and their life-styles.

Such a witness is not a burdened, strained obligation. It springs naturally out of the life lived in union with Christ. Such witness is ready to seize and buy up the opportunities as they come; to give answers with humility and love, to those who are seeking.

CONSISTENTLY (John 13:34, 35; Philippians 2:14-16; 1 Peter 3:15) Is your very lifestyle a witness for Christ? What is needed for your witness to never become a strained obligation?

Witnessing personally

When the early church experienced its first persecution, the believers were scattered throughout Judea and Samaria—all except for the apostles. Although these Christians were without the leadership of the apostles, we learn that they went everywhere, witnessing of Christ.

It was a matter of standing out in unashamed and personal testimony. Earlier the apostles had declared that it was impossible for them to keep silent about Christ. When we are living close to the love of God, we find that we cannot keep the good news to ourselves.

PERSONALLY (Acts 8:1, 4; Acts 4:18-20; Psalm 40:10) Is it possible for you to keep silent about Christ? What would encourage your witness to become bold and spontaneous?

Witnessing collectively

There is great strength and encouragement for all who join in combined witness. Jesus recognized the need to send His disciples out two by two. On the day of Pentecost, as Peter rose to proclaim Christ, his eleven companions stood with him. The book of Acts repeatedly tells us that the first Christians worked together.

Here was a unity in proclamation—a characteristic of any church which is working *with* Christ.

COLLECTIVELY (Acts 2:14, 42-47; Philippians 1:27) Is your church a collective witness for Christ? What can you do to encourage its witness?

Reflection Point: *Witnessing should never be a burdensome Christian duty, but the grateful privilege of those who have an experience of Jesus Christ. Review your notes from this lesson and write a sentence summarizing the ways to keep your witness for Christ fresh and alive.*

Thought Starters

1. Read the story of Philip and the Ethiopian official in Acts 8:26-40. What can we learn from Philip about bringing others to Jesus Christ? What qualities do we see in Philip? How prepared was the official for this encounter?

2. Which is easier—to speak to a stranger or to an acquaintance about Christ? Which seems to be more effective, and why?

3. Read 1 Thessalonians 2:7-13. List the qualities of Paul in this passage—his motive, his efforts, his persistence. How should these verses affect our way of spreading the good news?

4. Bearing in mind your gifts, what is there that you can do, naturally and freely, to help make Christ better known?

FURTHER STUDY

From your study of this lesson, determine two topics you could study further which would encourage and strengthen your witness for Christ. Beside each topic, give at least one Scripture verse you will use to begin your study.

"Let your light shine before men, that they may see your good deeds and praise your Father in heaven" (Matthew 5:16). On the Solent, England

THE CHRISTIAN AND THE WORLD

The Key Truth *The Christian has been called out of the world to be holy, but also he has been sent into the world for service and evangelism.*

THE CHRISTIAN IS

Called out of the world

"The world" means both this present, temporary *age*, and the hostile *system* of thought and action that operates on this planet. This is our environment.

But the Christian's true home is not here. Whatever our physical situation—good or bad—all that we value most strongly (our heavenly Father, Jesus Christ, our inheritance, our hope) is elsewhere. The New Testament urges Christ's followers to set their hearts on the eternal and heavenly dimension.

> *CALLED (1 Corinthians 7:29-31; Hebrews 10:32-34; Colossians 3:1, 2) How should this truth affect the way we view the world's circumstances?*

Separated from the world

This thread runs through most of the New Testament letters. Christians, because of their heavenward calling, are to avoid the trends and evil associations of fallen society. Their ethical standards are to be the highest of all.

Separation, however, does not mean that the Christian is called to withdraw from society, but to be kept committed to Christ within it.

> *SEPARATED (James 4:4, 5; Ephesians 5:3-11; John 17:15, 16) How should this truth affect the way we associate with and relate to people in the world?*

Sent into the world

The appeal of the New Testament is not simply that Christ's disciples should avoid being polluted by the world; rather they are to purify it. The Christian's attitude to the world should never be one of contempt. It is God's world, and we are to be involved in its redemption.

SENT (John 20:21; Matthew 5:13-16; John 3:16, 17) Review your two previous responses. How should this truth affect our involvement in the world?

To overcome the world

We must avoid judgmental views that simply dismiss the world as beyond the reach and care of God. But on the other hand, we should not fall into the trap of believing that the world is morally, socially or politically perfectible, however much may be done by Christians and others of good will to alleviate its problems. The true redemption of the world cannot be completed until the future glory of Christ is revealed.

Thus, the Christian is called upon to overcome the evil tendencies and pressures that the world brings to bear upon him. We are caught in a spiritual battle that involves every Christian in this dark age, and therefore we must be armed with spiritual weapons. Christ Himself has given us the assurance of His strength for the fight, and of the ultimate victory of God over all evil.

TO OVERCOME (Romans 8:19-21; Ephesians 6:10-18; Romans 8:37) How can we remain separated from the world and still be actively involved in helping overcome it?

To journey through the world

The Christian is a citizen of heaven, with relationships and privileges that are outside this world. We are like the Old Testament Jews, journeying toward a promised land, confident in the assurance of God's presence and guidance.

The pilgrim is required to exercise obedience and discipline. At times we are likened to a soldier who cannot afford to get entangled in civilian pursuits—or to an athlete who must observe the necessary rules. Our Christian life is the story of a pilgrimage through a world that is staggering under its problems. But we travel on with faith as our lamp.

TO JOURNEY (Philippians 3:20; Joshua 1:9; Hebrews 11:16) As a Christian, God is present with us and guides us as we journey through the world. How can we know and follow His guidance?

Reflection Point: *A true understanding of the world that God loves will strengthen the Christian's calling to go into all the world and proclaim Christ to every person. The world is evil, but its inhabitants have great need of Christ. Review your notes of this lesson and decide what your responses to others should be in the future.*

Thought Starters

1. Read and study 2 Timothy 4:1-22. Paul is in prison, nearing the end of his pilgrimage in Rome. How does he view the current scene, his own situation and future, and his acquaintances? Contrast the careers of Demas and Mark (compare with Acts 15:37-39).

2. The Christian cannot regard the present world system as perfectible. How can we avoid adopting either a judgmental attitude that writes the world off, or an extreme optimism that ends in disillusionment?

3. Read John 16:33. Why did Jesus encourage His disciples by saying these words? What do they mean for them—and us?

4. How can we keep our eternal goals clearly in view?

FURTHER STUDY

From your study of this lesson, list two aspects of your "relationship" with the world that you would like to study further. Beside each, give at least one scripture verse you will use to begin your study.

"Do not love the world or anything in the world" (1 John 2:15). New York City and the Hudson River

THE CHRISTIAN LIFE

The Key Truth *A Christian is a new being in Christ, reaching full potential as progress in life and faith is made. The Christian life is seen in these ways:*

A vocation to be fulfilled

The New Testament overflows with phrases that speak of goals, aims and ambitions. The apostle Paul alone is an example. He wants to finish his course; he desires to win the approval of God; he longs to proclaim Christ to those who have never heard of Him. All his ambitions were centered in Christ Himself, who was to have first place in everything.

All Christians have a calling—to be God's own people. Such a vocation overrides all other callings in life and, indeed, enhances them.

> *VOCATION (Philippians 3:14; Romans 15:20; Colossians 1:18) What are some of the ideas you have concerning how you will fulfill your vocation as God's own?*

A character to be developed

God's purpose for His people is that they should become like His Son Jesus Christ in the holiness of their living. To be a Christian does not mean only to believe in certain facts about Christ. Rather, it means to develop a Christ-like character. The Christian is to co-operate in this process, combating sinful habits and attitudes through the power of the Holy Spirit.

> *CHARACTER (Romans 8:29; 2 Peter 1:5-8; Ephesians 5:1, 2) In what ways have you seen God developing a Christ-like character in you?*

A fellowship to be maintained

The Christian is given ways and means by which the relationship with Christ may be maintained. Two examples of this are prayer and the Lord's supper.

The apostle John's first letter has much to say about the fellowship of the Christian life. It is a fellowship of *life*, for it centers in Christ, the Word of life. It is a fellowship of *love*, for all who are connected to Christ are connected also to each other. It is a fellowship of *light*, for there can be no darkness or hidden impurity where God is involved.

> *FELLOWSHIP (1 John 1:1-7; Ephesians 4:3-6; John 15:4) In what ways do you see your personal faith being a fellowship of life, a fellowship of love and a fellowship of light?*

Energies to be harnessed

God has given us many natural gifts. When we become Christians we are not to give up these abilities. Instead, motivated by the truths of our faith, we are to devote them to God's use, that they may reach their full potential and power.

The quality of daily work, our relationships and service will be heightened by the dynamic of Christ's resurrection power. We should recognize that we are not placed on this earth simply for ourselves. We are to be used by God.

ENERGIES (1 Corinthians 15:58; Ephesians 2:10; Colossians 3:23, 24) Have you seen God begin to use your natural abilities for His glory? How can you ensure their use for His good?

Minds to be developed

A Christian framework of thinking enables an individual to establish his relationship to the universe—simply because Christianity is true. By opening our intellects to the truth of God, we can be convinced about the deepest issues of life.

Each Christian must see to it that his mind is stretched to the limits of its capacity. Paul described those who were swept about with every shifting belief as "babies". His prayer was that the minds of younger Christians might be illuminated fully by the light of Christ. They were to be adult in their understanding.

MINDS (1 John 5:20; Ephesians 4:13, 14; Ephesians 1:18) What encouragement can you give to Christians whose only defense for their faith is that Christ has changed their lives?

A hope to be realized

It is the historic nature of the Christian faith—culminating in the resurrection of Jesus—that gives to God's people the eager expectation of their final inheritance in glory. The One who was raised will surely return; the past is forgiven; the present is covered, and tomorrow belongs to us.

HOPE (1 Peter 1:3-9; Titus 2:13; Revelation 22:20) When you think of living in glory with God, what specific thoughts do you have?

Reflection Point: *It is vital that Christ's followers should make not merely converts, but disciples, men and women of mature character and sound judgment. Name some ways you see God maturing you. How can you make mature believers from persons God allows you to encourage and help grow?*

Thought Starters

1. Read John 15:1-17. Reflect on what it means to be united with Jesus Christ. How is this achieved? What are Christ's expectations of His people? What are the privileges and challenges of this relationship?

2. Bertrand Russell (who was an atheist) once said of Christianity: "There is nothing to be said against it, except that it is too difficult for most of us to practice sincerely." How accurate is this assessment? Give your reasons.

3. How does your Christian faith affect your daily work? Discuss this with your friends.

4. How would you describe your relationship with Jesus Christ?

FURTHER STUDY
From your study of this lesson, list two topics you would like to study further. Beside each topic, give at least one Scripture verse from this or another study that you will use to begin your study.

"The life I live in the body, I live by faith in the Son of God, who loved me and gave Himself for me" (Galatians 2:20). Snowdonia, North Wales